HOW DID WE FIND OUT

ABOUT GENES?

The "HOW DID WE FIND OUT"... SERIES,
by Isaac Asimov

HOW DID WE FIND OUT—

HOW DID WE FIND OUT

ABOUT GENES?

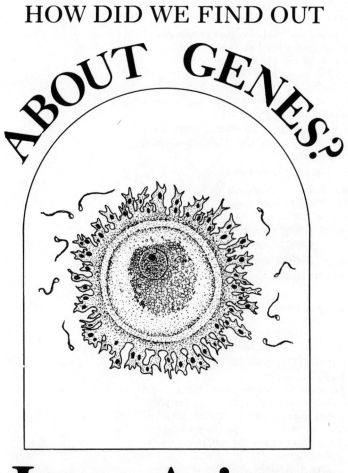

Isaac Asimov
Illustrated by David Wool

WALKER AND COMPANY
NEW YORK

First published in the United States of
America in 1983 by the Walker Publishing
Company, Inc.
This edition printed in 1985.
Published simultaneously in Canada by
John Wiley & Sons Canada, Limited,
Rexdale, Ontario.
ISBN: 0-8027-6499-1 Trade
        0-8027-6500-9 Reinforced
Library of Congress Catalog Card
Number: 83-1211

**Library of Congress Cataloging in
Publication Data**
Asimov, Isaac, 1920–
    How did we find out about genes?
    ("How did we find out" series)
    Includes index.
    Summary: Traces the developing
knowledge about heredity from the plant
breeding experiments of Gregor Mendel
to the use of x rays to produce mutations
and the effect of natural mutations on the
evolution of species.
    1. Genetics—History—Juvenile
literature. 2. Geneticists—Biography—
Juvenile literature.
    [1. Genetics] I. Wool, David, ill.
II. Title. III. Series: Asimov, Isaac,
1920–   . How did we find out—series.
QH428.A77 1983   575.1'09   83-1211
ISBN 0-8027-6499-1
ISBN 0-8027-6500-9 (lib. bdg.)
Printed in the United States of America
10 9 8 7 6 5 4 3 2

Dedicated to:
The Williams Family,
Hal
Pam
Gillian
Jeremy
Jessica
Benjamin

Contents

1 Mendel and Pea Plants

WE ALL KNOW that children usually resemble their parents. A child will have some features like those of its father, others like those of its mother. Brothers or sisters will often look alike.

Tall parents will have tall children; blue-eyed parents will have blue-eyed children; black-skinned parents will have black-skinned children.

These *physical characteristics* are *inherited.*

This is true not only of human beings, but also of animals and plants. Young living things resemble their parents. An oak tree does not give birth to a giraffe, and an oyster does not give birth to a dandelion. For that matter, two beagles do not give birth to a spaniel.

How does inheritance take place in such a way that physical characteristics are passed on from parents to their young?

It is hard to tell in human beings. In the first place,

GREGOR JOHANN MENDEL 1822–1884

there are so many different characteristics that it is hard to keep track of all of them. Then, too, it takes a long time for children to grow up so that you can study their characteristics and compare them to those of their parents. It would also help to have a great number of children so that you could study many cases, and a single pair of human beings don't really have enough of them.

Finally, you can't actually experiment. You can't try to arrange to have a man with a long nose marry a woman with a short nose in order to see what the noses are like in their children. You can't then arrange to have a man with a short nose marry a woman with a long nose to see if that makes a difference. You just have to look around for those people who are already married and try to find interesting cases among them. That can take a long, long time.

Over a century ago, though, an Austrian monk named Gregor Johann Mendel (MEN-del, 1822–1884) had an idea.

What Mendel really wanted was to be a high school teacher, but he had to pass an examination for that job, and he failed three times. He was very disappointed, but he decided he would feel better if he devoted himself to his hobby, which was botany, the study of plants.

That was when an idea came to him. In 1857, he decided that breeding plants was the best way to study the inheritance of physical characteristics. For one thing, plants stay put, so you can control them easily.

Then, too, you can easily control plant breeding. Plants produce sex cells in the flower. At the center of most flowers there is a *pistil* containing an *egg cell* in the *ovule*. You can take *pollen* (containing a sperm cell)

11

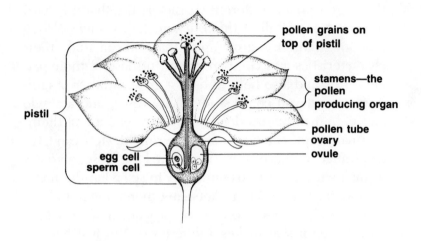

pollen grains on
top of pistil

stamens—the
pollen
producing organ

pistil

pollen tube
ovary
ovule

egg cell
sperm cell

CROSS-SECTION OF A FLOWER

from one plant and put it on the pistil of another plant, in any combination you wish. This is *cross-pollination*. When the pollen lands on the top of the pistil it grows a tube down which the sperm cell travels. It unites with the egg cell in the ovule in a process called *fertilization*. After fertilization, the ovules develop into seeds which can be planted and which will quickly grow. Then you can compare the characteristics of the new plants with the old ones that produced the pollen grains and the ovules.

In fact, you can take the pollen from a particular plant and put it on a pistil of the same plant (*self-pollination*). The seeds that would be produced in this way would have but one parent that was both father and mother. That could simplify things.

MENDEL'S GARDEN IN BRÜNN, AUSTRIA

For eight years, Mendel pollinated pea plants in different ways and studied the results.

As an example, he started with pea plants that were quite short when they were full-grown—only about one and one-half feet high. He self-pollinated a large number of them, and once the seeds were formed, he planted them. Every one of the seeds that he planted grew into a short pea plant. The short pea plants *bred true*.

He also worked with pea plants of a different variety that grew to be quite tall—six to seven feet high. He self-pollinated a large number of them and then planted the seeds. He found that some of those tall pea plants produced seeds that grew into tall pea plants

13

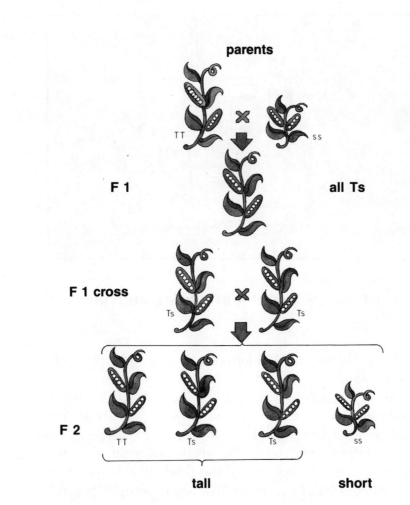

parents

F 1   all Ts

F 1 cross

F 2

tall   short

CROSSES OF TALL AND SHORT PEA PLANTS

every time. They also bred true. Other tall pea plants, however, produced seeds that did *not* breed true when they were self-pollinated. About three-quarters of their seeds grew to be tall pea plants, but one-quarter grew into short pea plants.

Mendel was astonished. All the tall pea plants looked exactly alike so far as height was concerned. Why should some breed true and some not?

He tried another experiment. This time he cross-pollinated He took the pollen from tall pea plants that bred true and put it on the pistils of short pea plants. He also took pollen from short pea plants and put it on the pistils of tall pea plants. The seeds that formed would have two parents, one tall and one short. Would some of the plants be tall and some short, or would they all be medium height?

Again Mendel was astonished, for neither of those things happened. There were no short pea plants and no medium-height pea plants. Every last seed, even though it was from one tall and one short plant, grew into a tall pea plant. Each one was just as tall as it would have been if both the pollen grains and the ovules had come from tall pea plants. The shortness characteristic had simply disappeared.

Mendel then took these tall pea plants he had grown and self-pollinated them. None of them bred true! Of the seeds they produced, about three-quarters grew into tall plants, and one-quarter into short plants.

The shortness characteristic had not disappeared after all. It had just hidden for one generation and then appeared in the next.

Mendel explained this by supposing that every plant had two factors inside itself that controlled the inheritance of a particular physical characteristic—one contributed by each parent. (What exactly those factors might be, Mendel didn't know, of course.)

The factor that brought about tallness could be called T and the factor that brought about shortness could be called s.

A short plant would have two s's, so that we could describe it as ss. Each sperm cell produced by an ss plant could have one of the two factors and so would have an s. In the same way, each egg cell would have an s.

When a sperm cell from a short pea plant combined with an egg cell from a short pea plant, the seed would receive an s from the sperm cell and another s from the egg cell. The seed would be ss and would grow into a short pea plant. This would happen to all short pea plants, and they would breed true.

A tall pea plant might have two factors for tallness. It would be TT. Every sperm cell and egg cell it produced would be a T, and the combination would be TT, so that the seeds would grow into tall pea plants. Such tall pea plants would also breed true.

But suppose the sperm cell from a short plant were combined with an egg cell from a tall plant. A sperm cell s would combine with an egg cell T, and the seed formed would be sT. If the sperm cell from a tall plant were combined with the egg cell of a short plant, a sperm cell T would combine with an egg cell s to form a seed that would be Ts. Either way, sT or Ts, the

DOMINANT TRAITS   RECESSIVE TRAITS

 barley

beardless   **bearded**

 mice

normal   **waltzing**

tomatoes

2-chambered fruit   **many-chambered fruit**

 sheep

white wool   **black wool**

17

seeds would produce tall pea plants. The *T* would drown out the effect of the *s*. Tallness would be *dominant* (from a Latin word meaning "master") and shortness would be *recessive* (from a Latin word meaning "to draw back").

But suppose you were to take a tall plant that is *Ts* (or *sT*) and use it to produce new plants. It would produce sperm cells that contain one of the factors—either one. Half the sperm cells would be *T*, and half would be *s*. The same would be true of the egg cells; half would be *T* and half would be *s*.

If the sperm cells were allowed to combine with the egg cells, each sperm cell *T* would combine with either an egg cell *T* or an egg cell *s* to produce a seed that would be either *TT* or *Ts*. Each sperm cell *s* would combine with either an egg cell *T* or an egg cell *s* to produce a seed that would be either *sT* or *ss*.

Four kinds of seeds would be produced: *TT*, *Ts*, *sT*, and *ss*, all in equal quantities. The *TT*, *Ts*, and *sT* seeds would all grow to be tall pea plants, while the *ss* seeds would grow to be short pea plants. All together, three-quarters of the seeds would give rise to tall plants, and one-quarter to short plants. The *TT* plants and the *ss* plants would breed true; the *Ts* plants and the *sT* plants (both of them tall) would not breed true.

Mendel tested his pea plants for other characteristics and found that his explanation worked for those characteristics, too. He tried combinations of characteristics, studying plants that had green seeds and that grew tall, others that had green seeds and grew short, still others that had yellow seeds and grew tall, and, finally, some that had yellow seeds and grew short. He found that he could explain which would breed true in both characteristics at once and which would not, and what proportions of all the different kinds he would get.

Once Mendel had it all worked out, he realized that scientists might not listen to him. After all, he was just a monk who was an amateur botanist, and he hadn't even passed the test that would have enabled him to be a teacher in a high school.

He thought, therefore, that he had better send a copy of the paper he wrote to some important professional botanist. If that botanist thought Mendel's work was worthwhile, he would sponsor it, and then scientists would listen.

Mendel sent it to a Swiss botanist, Karl Wilhelm von Nägeli (fon-NAY-guh-lee, 1817–1891). Von Nägeli was one of the most important botanists in Europe, and he must have been getting a great deal of mail from people of all sorts who wanted to interest him in their ideas. Probably, von Nägeli glanced casually at Mendel's work and thought: just another amateur.

He sent the material back to Mendel, who was terribly discouraged. In 1865 and 1869, Mendel managed to get his papers published in a respectable scientific journal, but not a really large one. Since no one sponsored the papers, other botanists paid no attention to them.

Mendel was so discouraged that he never did any more breeding experiments. He became abbot of his monastery in 1868 and devoted himself entirely to his monastery work. He died in 1884, not knowing that he would someday be famous. Von Nägeli died in 1891, never dreaming that he had made a terrible mistake and that despite all his scientific work, he would be remembered most of all for not having paid attention to Mendel.

But then, for over thirty years after Mendel's papers were published, no one else paid attention to him, either.

2 De Vries and Mutations

THE INHERITANCE OF physical characteristics does not always proceed as expected. Plants and animals do not always produce young that completely resemble themselves.

Every once in a while, young plants or animals are born that are different from their parents, and from their brothers and sisters. It is as though something has gone wrong with whatever it is that controls heredity.

Often it is clear that something has really gone wrong, because the young plant or animal is all distorted, one way or another, and doesn't live long. There may be two-headed calves, and other deformities. They were once called *sports*, as though nature was playing a grim sort of game.

In days past, many people thought that such a distorted birth was a warning from supernatural powers. Since the birth was "against nature," it might well be

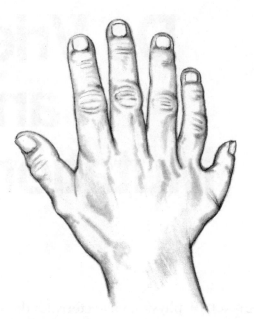

HUMAN HAND WITH SIX FINGERS—A MUTATION

that other things could happen that were also against nature. Nervous people expected evil things to be on the way. Sports were therefore also called *monsters*, from a Latin word meaning an "omen" or "warning."

Sports were chiefly noticed among domestic animals, but only farmers and herdsmen paid attention, and usually they died or were killed. When sports occurred in human births, they were usually hidden away, and often died.

Scientists generally paid no attention to them, even though some sports were useful.

In 1791, for instance, a Massachusetts farmer named Seth Wright discovered that one of his sheep had given birth to a lamb with very short legs. It was healthy in all other ways. When the lamb grew up, he was unable to jump over the fences with his short legs, so he was forced to stay in the pasture.

SHEEP WITH SHORT LEGS

23

Wright saw that this would be useful, since he didn't have to worry about that particular sheep getting out of the pasture and having to be chased. He bred the sheep and found that this resulted in other short-legged lambs. In a few years, he had a whole herd of such sports.

Eventually the herd died out, but another short-legged sport showed up in Norway, and again such herds were developed. Even so, that didn't seem to attract the attention of scientists who might be interested in heredity.

But then, in 1886, a Dutch botanist, Hugo de Vries (duh-VREEZ, 1848–1935) noticed something interesting.

HUGO DE VRIES AND HIS PRIMROSES

An American plant, the evening primrose, had been introduced into the Netherlands, and de Vries came across a colony of these plants growing in an unused meadow. They must all have grown from the seeds of a particular plant that had somehow taken root there, and yet de Vries could see at once that some of them were quite different from the others.

The different ones were sports, but they were quite able to grow and flourish. He dug up some and brought them back to his own garden, where he experimented with them quite as Mendel had done with his pea plants (though, at the time, de Vries knew nothing about Mendel).

De Vries found that while seeds from the evening primroses usually produced plants just like the plant that had produced the seeds, every once in a while the new plant was quite different from the old. De Vries called such a sudden change in heredity a *mutation*, from a Latin word for "change." Since then, scientists don't speak of sports or monsters, but only of mutations.

In his work, de Vries noticed the same things that Mendel had noticed. He gathered figures carefully, to show what proportion of plants had a particular characteristic and what proportion another characteristic. Like Mendel, he found that to explain his observations, he had to assume that each plant contained two factors controlling each physical characteristic, that one factor was present in the pollen grains and one in the ovules, and that these combined with each other according to chance.

By 1900, de Vries was ready to publish his work, to describe his *laws of inheritance*.

Two other botanists, unknown to de Vries and to each other, had also worked out the same laws of inheritance, and both of them were also ready to publish in 1900. They were a German botanist, Karl Erich Correns (KAWR-enz, 1864–1933) and an Austrian botanist, Erich Tschermak von Seysenegg (CHER-mahk-fon-ZY-zenek, 1871–1962).

Each one of these three botanists, before publishing his work, looked through earlier scientific journals to see what had already been done in the field. Imagine the amazement of each one when he came across Mendel's papers and saw that Mendel had figured out the laws of inheritance exactly as he had. Only Mendel had done it nearly forty years before.

All three botanists, de Vries, Correns, and Tschermak von Seysenegg, published their papers in 1900, but each one gave full credit to Mendel. That is why we now speak of the *Mendelian laws of inheritance* and why Mendel is now famous. Of course, he was dead long before his work was rediscovered.

3 Flemming and Chromosomes

MEANWHILE, THROUGHOUT THE 1800s, scientists were looking at various parts of plants and animals. They used microscopes in order to see all the tiny details. They kept noticing structures in living organisms that were too small to be seen except with a microscope, and these structures they called *cells*.

Cells were more clearly seen in plants than in animals. In 1838, a German botanist, Matthias Jakob Schleiden (SHLY-den, 1804–1881), announced that all plants were made up entirely of cells, which were separated from each other by thin walls. He said that cells were the building blocks of plant life.

The next year, a German biologist, Theodor Schwann (SHVAHN, 1810–1882) broadened the idea. He said that all animals, as well as all plants, were made up of cells, and that in animals they were separated from each other by even thinner membranes. Schleiden and

27

Schwann had thus advanced what came to be called the *cell theory* of life, and it turned out that they were correct.

In 1845, a German biologist, Karl von Siebold (ZEE-bohlt, 1804–1885), showed that microscopic living things could even be made up of a single cell.

Any living thing large enough to be seen with the naked eye is made up of a number of cells of different kinds, and is called a *multicellular organism*. The larger the organism, the greater the number of cells. Multicellular organisms grow by adding to the number of cells that make them up, and every one of them started as a single cell. In animals and plants the original single cell is an egg cell.

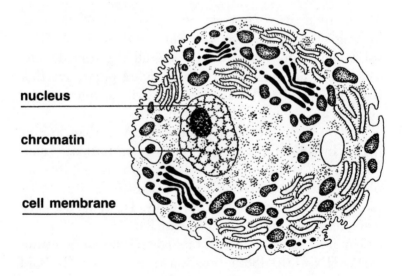

nucleus

chromatin

cell membrane

ANIMAL CELL

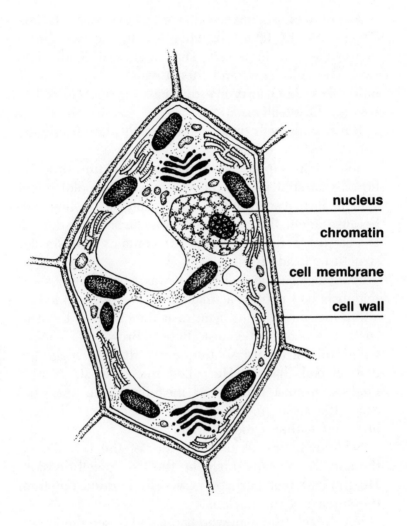

nucleus

chromatin

cell membrane

cell wall

PLANT CELL

29

A human being contains about 50 trillion (50,000,000,000,000) cells when it is fully grown, but it begins life as a single cell. That single cell divides into two. The cells grow and then divide in two again. It only takes about forty-five divisions for a single cell to become fifty trillion.

But how do cells divide? What takes place inside the cell during the division?

You might suppose that cells are just tiny drops of liquid that split in two the way a water droplet might split to form two droplets. That can't be so, however, because under the microscope you can see that the cell is not just a drop of liquid. It contains still smaller structures inside itself.

Even before the cell theory was worked out, some scientists had noticed a small structure, surrounded by a thin membrane of its own, near the center of the cell. In 1831, a Scottish botanist, Robert Brown (1773–1858), found this structure so frequently that he suggested that all cells had it. He called the small structure a *nucleus*, from a Latin word meaning "little nut," because the structure lay at the center of the cell like a little nut within a roomy shell.

Schleiden, one of the founders of the cell theory, thought the nucleus might be the key to cell division. He thought that perhaps new cells budded out from the surface of the nucleus.

Von Nägeli (the man who had failed to see the importance of Mendel's work) showed in 1846 that this was not so. Still, the nucleus had to be involved in cell division somehow. If a cell is divided into two pieces, and if one piece has the nucleus while the other does not, the piece without the nucleus dies. The piece of the cell *with* the nucleus recovers, grows, and continues to divide.

Yet how were scientists ever going to find out just what happened during the division? The contents of the cell are transparent. Whatever is seen looks like a dim shadow. Magnification doesn't help much here. It just makes the shadow bigger, but the details still don't really show.

In the 1850s and afterward, however, chemists were learning to produce all kinds of chemicals that weren't found in nature. In particular, they worked hard to produce colored chemicals: chemicals that could be used to dye textiles in brilliant colors that wouldn't wash out or fade in the sunlight. Dyes became a huge new industry.

It occurred to some biologists that cells could be dyed as well. If there were all sorts of different structures inside a cell, they might have different chemical makeups. Some particular dye might combine with some structures but not with others. Then, under the microscope, some parts of the cell's interior might be brightly colored, and other parts might not be. In that way, the interior could be studied more easily.

During the 1870s, a German biologist, Walther Flemming (1843–1905), used dyes in this way. He found one dye that was absorbed by certain regions inside the nucleus but by nothing else in the cell. Under the microscope, those regions could therefore be seen easily.

Flemming called the material inside the nucleus, which absorbed the dye, *chromatin* (KROH-muh-tin), from a Greek word for "color".

31

What Flemming did next was to look at a section of rapidly growing tissue under the microscope. Most of the cells were at different stages of cell division, as one would expect since it was growing, but nothing was clearly visible without the dye.

Flemming dyed the tissue and then put it under the microscope. Of course, the dye, in combining with material in the cell, poisoned the cells and killed them, so that the process of cell division did not actually continue. However, different cells were killed at different stages of cell division. It was like looking at different still pictures from a moving picture, in jumbled order. If you studied it hard enough, you could put all the stills into the right order and, in that way, figure out what was happening.

Flemming very carefully worked out the order of events in cell division and, in 1882, published a book in which he described all the details.

As the process of cell division begins, the chromatin material comes together within the nucleus and forms tiny rods, like stubby bits of microscopic spaghetti. Flemming called each of these rods a *chromosome* (KROH-moh-sohm), from Greek words meaning "colored body." Of course, chromosomes show no color naturally, but they were colored after being exposed to Flemming's special dye.

As cell division continues, each chromosome forms another one just like itself, so that each one is doubled.

Then the membrane of the nucleus seems to melt away. All the double chromosomes gather near the center of the cell and then move apart. Of each double chromosome, one moves toward one end of the cell and

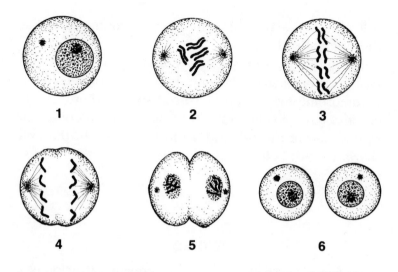

MITOSIS SHOWING THE FORMATION AND DIVISION OF CHROMOSOMES

the other toward the opposite end. In this way, there is a complete set of chromosomes at each end of the cell.

A membrane appears around each set of chromosomes so that a new nucleus is formed at each end of the cell. The cell then pinches together at the center and separates. There are then two cells, each with its own nucleus.

Others continued Flemming's work. One of them was a Belgian biologist named Edouard von Beneden (beh-NAY-den, 1846–1910).

In 1887, Beneden showed that all the cells in a particular type of plant or animal always have the same number of chromosomes. In cell division, this number is first doubled, so that after a division each daughter cell always has the same number of chromosomes as the original cell had.

For instance, we now know that every human cell has 46 chromosomes. When a human cell divides, each chromosome forms one like itself so that there are 92 chromosomes in the cell. 46 of these chromosomes go to one end of the cell and 46 to the other. In the end there are two cells, each with 46.

MEIOSIS

reduction division of a male primary sex cell

reduction division of a female primary sex cell

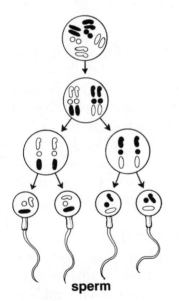

sperm

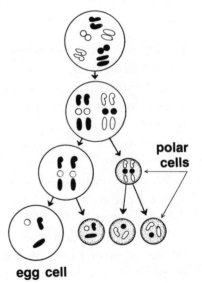

polar cells

egg cell

When sex cells are formed, each gets only *half a set of chromosomes*. This process is called meiosis and the division that takes place is called a reduction division. This means that in plants and animals, sperm cells and egg cells have only half the normal number of chromosomes. Thus, in human beings, though there are 46 chromosomes in each cell, sperm cells and egg cells have only 23 chromosomes.

When a human sperm cell combines with a human egg cell, the 23 chromosomes of one are added to the 23 chromosomes of the other. The result is a "fertilized egg cell" containing 46 chromosomes, half from the father and half from the mother.

As the fertilized egg cell divides and divides and divides, every new cell that is formed has 46 chromosomes, half like those from the father and half like those from the mother.

4 Morgan and Fruit Flies

BIOLOGISTS DIDN'T SEE the real importance of the work of Flemming and Beneden until 1900, when de Vries, Correns, and Tschermak von Seysenegg rediscovered the Mendelian laws of inheritance. Then it was possible to see that the chromosomes fit the Mendelian laws perfectly.

The first to point this out was the American biologist, Walter Stanborough Sutton (1877–1916). In 1902, when he was only twenty-five, he published a paper in which he showed that all the chromosomes existed in pairs which were very similar to each other in structure. Instead of thinking of human cells as containing 46 chromosomes, they should be thought of as containing 23 chromosome pairs.

Then, in 1903, he showed that sperm cells and egg cells have one of each pair of chromosomes. The 23 chromosomes they each have are a kind of half set. (It's

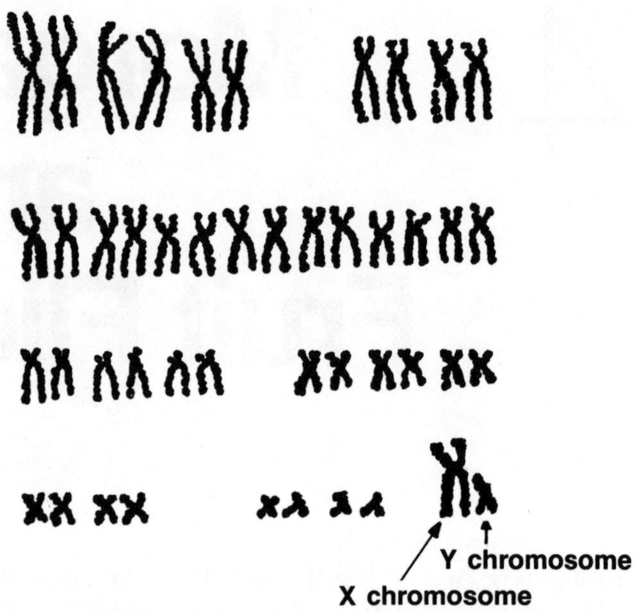

↑ Y chromosome
X chromosome

THE 46 CHROMOSOMES IN A HUMAN MALE BODY CELL IN 22 PAIRS + 2 SEX CHROMOSOMES

like imagining every cell as containing all the letters of the alphabet, both capital and small. In that case the sex cells would also have every letter of the alphabet, but only the capitals—or only the small letters.)

The fertilized egg cell has 23 chromosome pairs again, but of each pair, one comes from the father and one from the mother.

Think back to Mendel's pea plants.

Suppose there were a chromosome in the pea-plant cell that controlled tallness or shortness. That chromosome might be a *T* or an *s*. The chromosome would also have its partner, which would also help to control

38

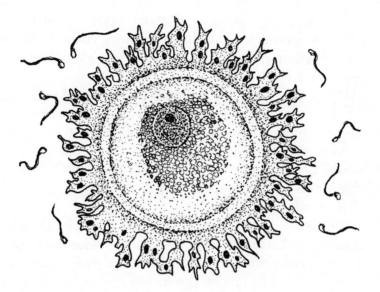

HUMAN SEX CELLS

tallness or shortness, and *it* would be a *T* or an *s* also. As a result, the chromosome pair would be *TT*, *Ts*, *sT*, or *ss*.

The sperm cell of a *TT* plant would always have just one chromosome of the pair and would be a *T.* The sperm cell of an *ss* plant would always have one chromosome of the pair and would always be a *s*. In the case of an *sT* plant or a *Ts* plant, the sperm cells would get one of the pair, so that half of them would be *s* and half would be *T*. The same would be true of the egg cells. If you imagine sperm cells and egg cells combining to form seeds, and remember that *T* is dominant over *s*, then all of Mendel's laws would work out.

It was truly amazing. Without knowing anything about chromosomes, and by just looking at the result of his pea-plant pollinations, Mendel had described exactly what chromosomes do.

Of course, there were bound to be some puzzling points. For one thing, there weren't enough chromosomes. Human cells have 23 pairs of chromosomes, but if each pair controlled one physical characteristic, that would be 23 characteristics, and that just isn't believable. Human beings inherit far more than 23 physical characteristics.

The answer to that problem is actually a simple one. It must be that small portions of each chromosome control particular characteristics. These portions occur all along the length of the chromosome, like beads on a string. There may be dozens, hundreds, even thousands of such portions on each chromosome.

In 1909, a Danish botanist, Wilhelm Ludvig Johannsen (yoh-HAN-sun, 1857–1927) suggested that each chromosome portion that controls a physical characteristic be called a *gene* (JEEN), from a Greek word meaning "to give birth to." The suggestion was adopted, and from then on everyone considered chromosomes to be strings of genes.

But there were other problems, too—harder ones. For instance, what produces males and females? Among human beings (and many other animals), half the children born are male and half are female. Maleness and femaleness are very important physical characteristics, yet they don't follow Mendelian laws. Mendelian laws show a new generation to possess all of one characteristic and none of the other, or to be divided up

CHROMOSOMES OF AN INSECT. ALONG THE
LENGTH OF EACH CHROMOSOME LIE SEVERAL
THOUSAND GENES.

3 to 1. At no time do they show a division of 1 to 1, as in maleness and femaleness.

This was one of the problems that interested an American biologist, Thomas Hunt Morgan (1866–1945). To investigate it, he began to make use, in 1908, of a small insect called a fruit fly. Its scientific name is *Drosophila* (droh-SOF-ih-luh). The advantages of using it were that it bred very quickly and produced many young. It was small and didn't require much room or much feeding, and its cells had only four pairs of chromosomes.

Fruit flies usually have red eyes, but occasionally Morgan came across one with white eyes. When Morgan put a white-eyed male with a red-eyed female in a bottle, all the offspring were red-eyed. That was to be expected by the Mendelian laws if red eyes were dominant over white eyes.

When Morgan bred the red-eyed offspring among themselves, the result was red eyes and white eyes in a 3 to 1 division. Again, this was what Mendelian laws predicted.

There was, however, a surprise! All the white-eyed flies were male! Why was that?

Morgan looked more closely at the chromosomes of the fruit fly. It turned out that the females had four perfect pairs. One of these pairs was what Morgan decided to call a pair of *X-chromosomes*. Male fruit flies had three perfect pairs, but had only one X-chromosome. There was no partner to it.

This meant that when a female fruit fly formed egg cells, each egg cell would have one of each chromo-

THOMAS HUNT MORGAN

red-eyed female   **red-eyed male**   **white-eyed male**

FRUIT FLIES

some pair, and each would therefore have one X-chromosome.

When male fruit flies formed sperm cells, each cell would have one of each of three chromosome pairs, but the X-chromosome would have no partner. That meant that half the sperm cells would have an X-chromosome and half would not.

If a fruit-fly egg cell combined with a sperm cell containing an X-chromosome, the fertilized egg cell would have two X-chromosomes and would develop into a female. If the egg cell combined with a sperm cell that did not contain an X-chromosome, the fertilized egg cell would have only one X-chromosome and would develop into a male.

Since the two types of sperm cells occur in equal numbers, half the fertilized egg cells would develop into males and half into females.

(This sort of thing also happens in human beings. Women have 23 perfect pairs of chromosomes in each

44

female　　　　　　　　　　**male**

CHROMOSOMES OF THE FRUIT FLY

cell. Men have 22 perfect pairs plus an X-chromosome, which has as its partner just a little stub called a Y-chromosome.)

How does this explain the reason why the white-eyed fruit flies were all males?

The gene that controls eye color in fruit flies is on the X-chromosome. A female fruit fly with a red-eye gene on both X-chromosomes (RR) has red eyes. Even if she has a white-eye gene on one of the chromosomes (Rw or wR), she has red eyes, for red eyes are dominant over white eyes. Only if there were a white-eye gene on each X-chromosome (ww) would a female have white eyes. However, the white-eye gene is quite rare, so to have it on both X-chromosomes is very rare indeed, and one hardly ever finds a female fruit fly with white eyes.

In males, there might be a red-eye gene on the single X-chromosome ($R0$), and it would then have red eyes. There might also be a male with a white-eye gene on the X-chromosome ($w0$), and it would have white eyes. One white-eye gene is enough, for there would be no second X-chromosome in a male that would carry a dominant red-eye gene.

Suppose a white-eyed male ($w0$) were mated with an ordinary red-eyed female (RR). Each egg cell would be R, but there would be two kinds of sperm cells, w and 0. Half the fertilized egg cells would get the X-chromosome with the w and would be Rw. They would all be females and would all have red eyes. The other half would get no X-chromosome and would be $R0$. These would all be males and would all have red eyes.

But what if these red-eyed offspring, female Rw and male $R0$, were mated among themselves? Half the egg cells would be R and half would be w. Either one of them might get an X-chromosome from the sperm cells and would then produce females. In that case, half the females would be Rw, half would be RR, and all would have red eyes.

On the other hand, the egg cells might get no X-chromosome from the sperm and would then produce males. In that case, half the males would be $R0$ and have red eyes, while half the males would be $w0$ and have white eyes. This means that one-quarter of all the offspring (half of the half that are male) would have white eyes and they would *all be males* exactly as Morgan observed.

Morgan described the eye-color characteristic in fruit flies as *sex-linked*. Sex-linkage can be important in human beings, too. Color blindness, for instance, is sex-linked in human beings. It is almost always males,

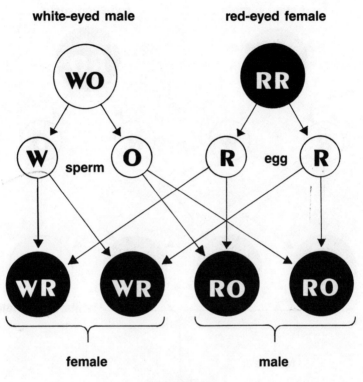

A CROSS BETWEEN A RED-EYED FEMALE AND A WHITE-EYED MALE

F 1 cross

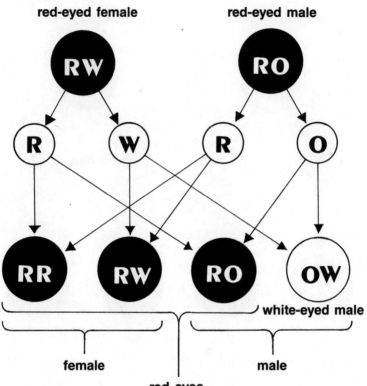

A CROSS BETWEEN MEMBERS OF THE F 1 GENER-
ATION

48

and hardly ever females, who are color-blind. And it is females who carry that characteristic in their genes without showing it, and who can pass it on to their sons (not to their daughters).

There are other kinds of linkage, too. Every time a chromosome is passed on from parent to child, a whole string of genes is passed on. Every characteristic controlled by each of these genes is passed on.

Thus, if some characteristic of fruit-fly wings and some characteristic of fruit-fly legs are on the same chromosome, they should always be inherited together. The young should always have either both or neither.

Morgan was able to show that this was exactly what happened in fruit flies, and by 1910 Sutton's suggestion was proven that the chromosomes were Mendel's factors. (Morgan won a Nobel Prize in 1933 for his work.)

Still, linkage is not perfect. Fruit flies might inherit characteristic *A* and characteristic *B* together over and over again, so it might seem beyond doubt that both characteristics were on the same chromosome—and then something would go wrong. There would always be a few fruit flies who would inherit characteristic *A*, but *not* characteristic *B*, or vice versa. Then, if those fruit flies that showed broken linkage were bred among themselves, the two characteristics would stay unlinked in their offspring.

Morgan could see what was happening. The chromosomes don't line up neatly at cell division like soldiers on parade. They look like a tangle of spaghetti. The two chromosomes of a pair are bent around each other and sometimes exchange parts. This is called *crossing-over*.

The part with the gene controlling characteristic *B*

might join the other member of the pair. The equivalent part of the second chromosome might join the first, which would then have a slightly different gene producing a somewhat different characteristic than the usual one. The egg cell or sperm cell gets a chromosome that contains the gene for characteristic A, but characteristic B is in a form slightly different from its accustomed form.

In 1911, Morgan discussed the crossing-over of chromosomes with a twenty-year-old student of his, Alfred Henry Sturtevant (STUR-tuh-vant, 1891–1970). Sturtevant had an exciting idea. If two genes were far apart on a chromosome, almost any crossover would separate them. A dividing line almost anywhere on the chromosome would do the trick.

If, on the other hand, two genes were close together on the chromosome, they would hardly ever be separated by crossing-over. The dividing line would have to

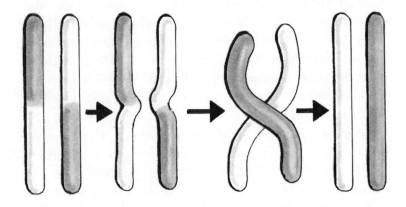

CROSSOVER OF CHROMOSOMES

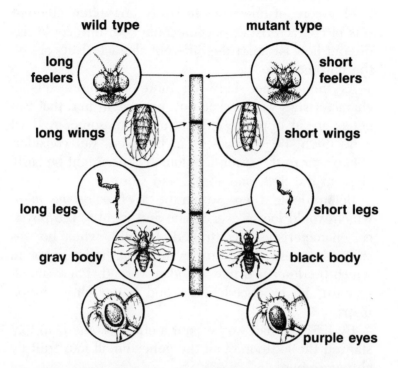

wild type   mutant type

long feelers   short feelers

long wings   short wings

long legs   short legs

gray body   black body

purple eyes

A SIMPLIFIED GENE MAP SHOWS THE POSITION OF CERTAIN GENES ON ONE OF THE FRUIT FLY'S CHROMOSOMES.

take place just between the two, and there wouldn't be much room for that.

Therefore, if one were to study how often different sets of characteristics become unlinked, one could figure out how far apart the different characteristics are on the chromosome.

As the distance between more and more sets of characteristics was worked out, one might find that two genes are at opposite ends of a chromosome. A third gene might be somewhere in between, but considerably closer to the second. A fourth gene might be fairly close to the first, and so on, and so on.

Before long, there would be a *chromosome map*, which would locate every gene and identify the physical characteristic it controlled. In 1913, when he was still only twenty-two, Sturtevant published a paper in which he described how his idea worked. For years afterward, he produced better and better chromosome maps.

By 1951, he had worked out a chromosome map that showed the location of all the genes on all four fruit fly chromosomes.

5 Muller and X-rays

Why should there be both a red-eye gene and a white-eye gene, each capable of being in the same position on a chromosome, so that one chromosome might have one and its pair might have the other? After all, the red-eye gene is the normal one for that characteristic; it is certainly the most common of the two. It must have been the one that existed to begin with, and at every cell division another red-eye gene must have been formed. Where, then, do the unusual white-eye genes come from?

The fact is that mutations do take place, as de Vries had shown.

De Vries had, however, worked only with plants, and the question arose as to whether animals undergo mutations, too. Certainly, there were many reports of mutations among domestic animals, like those short-legged sheep, but scientists would feel more comfortable if

53

they could study mutations in their own laboratories and not have to depend on reports from farmers and herdsmen.

Morgan, in his experiments with fruit flies, noticed that every once in a while a mutation would take place. For instance, he might start with red-eyed fruit flies that bred true. All their offspring would be red-eyed, and all the offspring of those offspring would be red-eyed, too. There would be no sign of white eyes anywhere.

But then, every once in a while, a white-eyed fruit fly would appear. Where did it come from?

Morgan had another student, Hermann Joseph Muller (1890–1967), who was particularly interested in this mutation problem. His notion was that each gene had to be made up of atoms in a very complicated arrangement. During cell division, each gene on each chromosome somehow has to produce another gene exactly like itself, with all the atoms precisely in place.

Most of the time, this was done, but it was only natural to suppose that every once in a while there would be a mistake. Some atoms would get out of place, and the gene that was produced wouldn't work quite in the way it was supposed to. It would be a different gene variety, and the color of the eye, or the shape of the wing, would be different as a result.

Anything that made it harder to keep the atoms in place, or that made it easier for them to get out of place, should then increase the number of mutations.

For instance, all atoms vibrate, or jiggle. This is the effect of the energy they contain. The higher the temperature, the greater the energy they contain, and the more rapidly they jiggle. Muller reasoned that if all the atoms were jiggling more rapidly than usual, it would be harder to produce a complicated gene with all the atoms exactly in place.

If this reasoning of Muller's was right, then mutations would increase if he kept the fruit flies at a slightly higher temperature than usual.

In 1919, Muller tried this, and he discovered that he was quite right. The number of mutations did go up with temperature.

It wasn't enough, though. The number didn't go up very much, and Muller couldn't improve things by continuing to raise the temperature. If he raised the temperature too much, the fruit flies would die. Was there something besides heat that would stir up the atoms and get in the way of a perfect duplication of a gene?

Only about a quarter of a century before, X-rays were discovered. These are a high-energy kind of radiation. If an X-ray hits a complicated set of atoms, it sets them all to quivering strongly—so strongly that the whole array might break apart. What's more, X-rays can penetrate matter so that they can reach the chromosomes inside the fruit fly very easily; they wouldn't be stopped at the skin.

It seemed to Muller that it would be much better to expose fruit flies to X-rays than to an increase in temperature. Increasing the temperature affected all the atoms without exceptions; X-rays affected only those atoms they struck. If X-rays hit a gene, the gene would be broken up, but the rest of the fruit fly's body would be left intact. That meant that he could add a great deal of energy to the chromosomes without killing the fruit fly altogether.

By 1926, it was clear that he had hit the bull's-eye. X-rays worked as he suspected they would. The mutation rate went way up.

This discovery was useful in that it supplied biologists with a great many mutations of all sorts, which they could use to study the details of inheritance, to map chromosomes, and so on. (Muller received a Nobel Prize in 1946 for this work.)

It also explained what makes X-rays and other energetic kinds of radiation so dangerous to people. It upsets the function of the chromosomes. From then on, Muller worked hard to warn people against using X-rays needlessly.

It showed, too, how it was that mutations took place under natural conditions.

All living things are constantly exposed to different kinds of energy. There are highly energetic particles called *cosmic rays* that constantly bombard the earth. There are energetic particles and radiation that arise from tiny amounts of radioactive atoms which are always present everywhere about us. There is even sunlight, and certain chemicals that occur around us naturally. All of these things can interfere with the perfect duplication of genes and all can work to produce different varieties of particular genes.

This means that every gene that human beings (and other living things, too) possess exists in many varieties. This makes heredity a far more complicated matter than it would be if every gene existed in one variety. Think of all the different shapes and sizes of noses; all the differences in hands, ears, height, coloring, teeth, voice, and so on. It is because of this variety that you can so easily recognize everyone you know by appearance, by voice, by manner of walking, and in many other ways.

Then, too, if there were no mutations so that all genes existed in a single variety, all members of a species would look alike.

As it is, every single living thing has its own mix of hundreds or thousands of genes and is different from every other. Among animals of a particular kind, some are faster, some are smarter, some can hide more easily, some can live better on a particular variety of food—all because each has its own complicated combination of genes.

This means that some individual animals can manage to survive more successfully than others of the same kind. Some varieties of genes, or combinations of varieties, are more useful in the long run. Other varieties are particularly useless and put their owners under such a disadvantage that they don't live long.

Useless genes tend to diminish in number as plants or animals that possess them die quickly. Those genes may never completely vanish, for new examples will turn up every once in a while as new mutations. They will not flourish, however.

Useful gene varieties that give an advantage to those living things that possess them will enable those particular creatures to live longer and better, and to have more children (many of whom will be likely to inherit that gene variety). Such a gene type will increase and become more and more common.

The way in which useful genes become more widespread, and useless genes less widespread, is called *natural selection*. Natural forces (the need of living things to compete with each other for food and mates and safety) select the useful gene varieties and makes them common.

Most mutations that take place result in rather poor gene varieties, and even very harmful ones. That doesn't matter. It is the very few useful mutations which increase and spread.

Each different kind of plant or animal experiences mutations and natural selection and therefore comes to fit its environment more and more efficiently. Enough changes might take place over a few million years to turn one kind of animal into a slightly different (and more efficient) kind, or into two or more different kinds.

There is a slow *evolution*, so that birds and mammals, for instance, gradually arose by slow stages,

HONEYCREEPER BIRDS WITH CURVED BILLS EVOLVED FROM A COMMON FINCH-LIKE ANCESTOR.

through random mutation and natural selection, from reptiles. From simple insect-eating mammals resembling present-day tree-shrews, such animals as lemurs, monkeys, and apes gradually developed.

Several million years ago, some rather primitive ape-like mammals split up into several varieties by way of random mutation and natural selection, and one of those varieties eventually developed into modern man.

Our present understanding of this process began, in part, because a monk couldn't pass the test that would have allowed him to serve as a teacher, so that he decided to interest himself instead in the growing and breeding of pea plants.

Index

Pollen, 11, 12

Recessive traits, 17, 18
Reduction division, 34

Schleiden, Matthias Jacob, 27
Schwann, Theodor, 27
Seeds, 12
Self-pollination, 12
Sex-linked characteristics, 46
Siebold, Karl von, 28
Sperm cells, 11, 12, 34ff. 44

Sports, 21
Sturtevant, Alfred Henry, 50
Sutton, Walter Stanborough, 37

Temperature, mutations and, 55
Tschermak von Seysenegg, Erich, 26

Wright, Seth, 23, 24

X-chromosome, 42ff.
X-rays, mutations and, 55, 56